GIVING THANKS

❦ *The 1621 Harvest Feast* ❦

by KATE WATERS

Photographs by RUSS KENDALL

In Cooperation with Plimoth Plantation

SCHOLASTIC PRESS • NEW YORK

❧ ACKNOWLEDGMENTS ❧

We acknowledge the staff of the Wampanoag Indian Program at Plimoth Plantation ™, especially Linda Coombs and Darrel Wixon and the members of the Wampanoag nations and other Native communities, including Narragansett, Nipmuc, Mohegan, Cherokee, Lakota, Aymara, Quechua, Montagnais, and Navajo, for recreating the events that allowed us to tell this story. We also acknowledge the staff of Plimoth Plantation, especially Liz Lodge, Kathy Roncarati, Maureen Richard, Kathleen Curtin, Carolyn Travers, Martha Sulya, Jill Hall, Lisa Whalen, Carol City, and Bill McAvoy. Additional thanks to Thérèse Landry, photographer's assistant.

TO OUR WONDERFUL CAST: Graham Lebica, who plays Resolved; Matt Boardley, who plays Dancing Moccasins; Darrel Wixon, who plays Dancing Moccasins's father; Moira Turnan Hannon, who plays Resolved's mother; Christian Hall, who plays Bartle; Annawon Weeden, who plays the messenger; David Goglia, who plays Resolved's stepfather; B.J. Rudder, who plays Uncle Gilbert Winslow; Rosario Gomez-Dunn, who plays Dancing Moccasins's mother; Wayra Gomez-Dunn, who plays Dancing Moccasins's brother; and Seaman Turner, who plays Massasoit.

LIBRARY OF CONGRESS CATALOGING-IN-PUBLICATION DATA

Waters, Kate. • Giving Thanks: The 1621 Harvest Feast / by Kate Waters ; photographs by Russ Kendall. • p. cm. • ISBN 0-439-24395-5 • 1. Thanksgiving Day—Juvenile literature. 2. Indians of North America—Massachusetts—Social life and customs—Juvenile literature. 3. Massasoit, 1580–1661—Juvenile literature. [1. Thanksgiving Day. 2. Indians of North America—Massachusetts. 3. Massasoit, 1580–1661.] I. Kendall, Russ, ill. II. Title. America—Massachusetts. 3. Massasoit, 1580–1661.] I. Kendall, Russ, ill. II. Title. • GT4975 .W38 2001 • 394.2649—dc21 • 00-050477 Printed in Singapore   46 • First edition, September 2001 • 10 09 08 07 06 05 04 03 02 01 01 02 03 04 05 • Book design by Nancy Sabato

To my brothers and sisters, Edward, Anne, Gregory,
Benedict, and Margaret, in thanks for special friendships.
—K. W.

To Stan Grossfeld, for his kindness early on.
—R. K.

Dancing Moccasins

Resolved White

AUTUMN 1621

Sometime between September 21 and November 9, 1621,

the English colonists, whom we call Pilgrims, and the

Wampanoag people shared a harvest celebration.

Through time, stories and popular myths have evolved

around this event, which has come to be known as the

first Thanksgiving. But this is the story of what

may have happened during those days, as told by

Dancing Moccasins, a 14-year-old Wampanoag boy,

and Resolved White, a 6-year-old English boy.

Dancing Moccasins

It is autumn and almost time for my family to move to our winter home.
Some of our corn and beans have been taken back to our village. Some will
be stored at the homesite until next spring. I helped dig the storage pits.
My little brother helps me carry a sack of corn to the pit. Our family has
dried some fish, and we will continue to hunt and fish during the winter.

I thank Kietan, our Creator, for the plentiful harvest and good hunting.

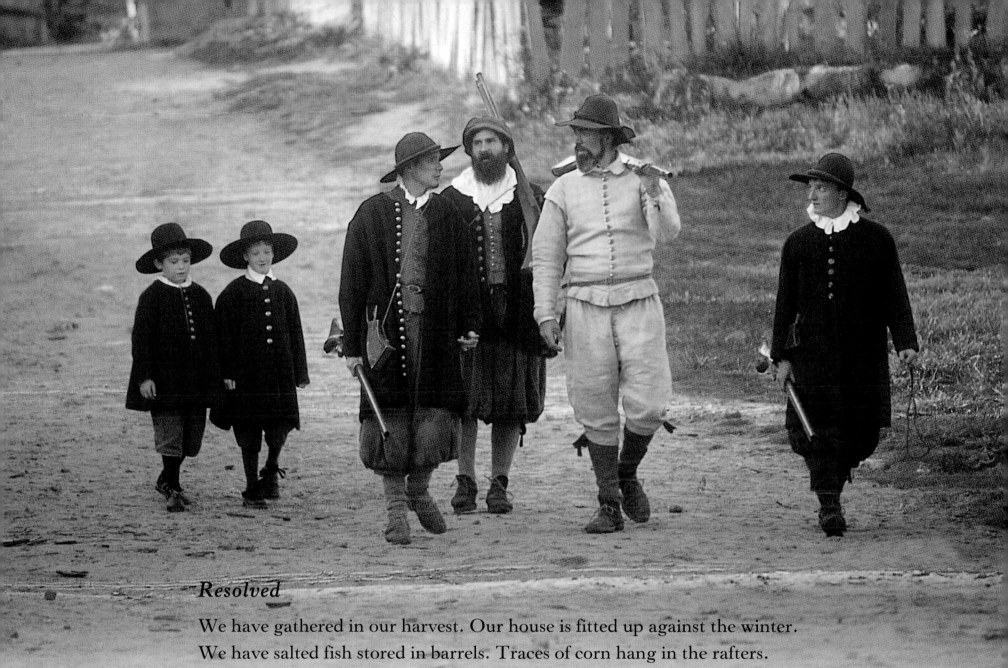

Resolved

We have gathered in our harvest. Our house is fitted up against the winter.
We have salted fish stored in barrels. Traces of corn hang in the rafters.

Now, it is time to celebrate. We will feast and play. We will rejoice that
the hard work of bringing in the harvest is finished and give thanks that the
harvest was plentiful. My mother says I can go to play stool ball with my
friend Bartle while she cooks. We follow my uncle Gilbert and other men
who are going fowling.

Dancing Moccasins

This morning I walk through the forest around our homesite looking for deer tracks. My father and grandfather will take deer for food and use the hides for new clothes and blankets for our family.

I hear constant musket fire in the distance. We often hear one or two shots but this is unusual. It has scared the deer away.

I go to the edge of the forest to see what the English are doing. I've seen them many times before but they have never noticed me. Today, some of the children are playing a game. A red-haired boy hits the ball and it lands near me.

Resolved

I throw the ball but miss the stool broadly. It lands near the feet of an
Indian boy who is standing at the edge of the forest. He throws the ball
back to me. I know him not but I give him greeting. He answers back in
his tongue. I see him surveying our men at arms and the cleared field.
I run to tell my friend Bartle, but when we look back, the boy has
disappeared into the forest. I wonder why he watches us?

Dancing Moccasins

I run right back to our homesite to report the activity in the English village.
I rarely see the English children playing. And the men are shooting at targets
instead of hunting animals.

I also tell my father about the deer yards I found at the edge of the forest.

Just then, a tall man comes up the path. He is a messenger from Massasoit bringing news that our *sachem* is journeying to visit the English. He wants Father to join the group in the morning. I wonder why Massasoit goes to visit the English?

Resolved

Although I watch the forest, the Indian boy does not show himself again.
Past midday, my uncle Gilbert comes out of the forest with many ducks.
He asks me to carry them home. Play is done for today. I sit outside to
pluck the fowl. Feathers fly all around.

A messenger from Pokanoket comes to our house and asks for my stepfather. I hear him say that Massasoit, his wife, and many men are on
their way to visit our village.

My stepfather is curious. "What is the purpose of King Massasoit's visit?" he wonders out loud.

Dancing Moccasins

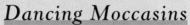

Father has said that I may join him and
travel with Massasoit and our people
tomorrow. I have never been into the
English village. I wonder how they will
greet us.

Resolved

Before sleep, I draw one more pail of water
for Mother. She is already preparing food
for tomorrow, when our governor will
entertain Massasoit at his table. I know not
whether to rejoice or fear for tomorrow.

Dancing Moccasins

At daybreak, Father and I set off toward the village. I run ahead to catch
up to Massasoit and his men.

Resolved

Since sunup, I have ground corn and fetched water.
Mother sends me to gather kindling at the edge of the
forest. Suddenly I see a mighty sight: Massasoit is here!
And there are many men with him.

Dancing Moccasins

When we reach the edge of the forest, I hear a drum. The English leader is coming to meet us. He bows to our *sachem*.

Resolved

King Massasoit greets Master Bradford, our governor. The musketeers
salute the visitors like royalty.

Dancing Moccasins

Massasoit sends several hunters to
get deer as a gift for the English.
Father sends me, too, since I
tracked deer nearby yesterday.

Resolved

Mother has gone to our governor's house to oversee dinner. I peek through the window and see my stepfather, Master Bradford, Massasoit, and other important men at the table. Their food is finer than any I've seen since leaving home.

Both the governor and the king give thanks for the food.

Dancing Moccasins

The hunt was successful. We have returned with five deer, which were given to the English.

I help set the fire pits and gather poles and firs to build our shelters. This is where we will eat and sleep during our visit.

Resolved

Some native children are playing a game. They are Hobbamock's family and live close to us. The boy I saw in the forest is with them!

Dancing Moccasins

Some of our young children are playing the pin game. The red-haired English boy is watching. I call to him and show him how to play. He is not very good at first, but this game takes practice.

Resolved

Later, I watch some of our men and some of the native men pitching the bar in the street. Each wants to be the strongest and throw the log farthest.

Resolved

As the sun lowers, I sup with some of the other village children and their families. There is venison and duck and goose and pompion and samp.

Dancing Moccasins

Father and I cook some venison and talk about this day. I am glad he allowed me to join him.

Dancing Moccasins

Later, Father leads the singing.
He uses singing sticks to keep
time.

Some of the men dance
to the songs. They do the
warrior's dance.

I can see the English boy
watching from the hill.

Resolved

Mother calls me home. I help her cook, since the celebration will last several days.

As swiftly as I can, I grind the corn for samp while mother roasts one of the ducks I plucked.

At last she allows me to walk down to where my uncle is standing watch. I listen to the singing and watch the dancing.

Dancing Moccasins

Everyone else is asleep. But I am excited to be away from home and among the men. This has been an eventful day for me.

I wonder what the next days will be like here among the English. I hope I can explore the village more. I thank Kietan for showing me the deer tracks and for my part in the successful hunt.

Wunniook. Be well.

Resolved

My stepfather fetches me home. I tell him about the boy who showed me the game. He says our visitors will be here for several days.

I say my prayers and give special thanks for these days of celebration. Perhaps I will spend time with my new friend tomorrow.

This is the most wondrous time since we arrived in this new land.

Good night. God keep you.

THE MYTH OF THE FIRST THANKSGIVING

On the fourth Thursday in November, many people in the United States celebrate a holiday called Thanksgiving. Most of us think we are continuing a tradition begun by the Pilgrims and the native Wampanoag. But the time-honored image of Pilgrims inviting Indians to share one meal is a myth. That is not what happened. This book tells and shows you what scholars think really happened. We have tried to present this event with a balanced point of view, from the eyes of a young English settler and an older Wampanoag boy.

Between 1616 and 1618, a great plague, carried by European fishermen and traders, struck the area from southern Maine to Narragansett Bay. The illness swept through the Wampanoag homeland, wiping out whole villages, including Patuxet. In November 1620, English colonists aboard the *Mayflower* arrived at Cape Cod and began searching for a place to settle. They chose Patuxet, already called Plimouth by English explorers, because it appeared to be uninhabited and was surrounded by cleared fields ready for planting. While continuing to live on board ship, they began to build houses on land. Weakened by the lengthy voyage and lack of shelter, half of the settlers died during that winter.

In the spring, the colonists planted crops. Their neighbor, Tisquantum, also called Squanto, helped them plant seeds from local plants. When the crops were harvested in the autumn, the settlers saw that they had enough food to last them through another winter.

At this time, Massasoit, the *sachem* of the Pokanoket village, decided to visit the English village. No one knows exactly why he chose this time for his visit. He had met the former governor, John Carver, and had traded many times with this group of English people and other traders before them. He and his wife and 90 men set out to visit the settlement. Massasoit journeyed from Pokanoket, known today as Bristol, Rhode Island. It was a two-day walk from there to the English village. His messenger could run the distance in one day. In the photograph on page 13, you will see that the messenger carries a copper chain. This signifies that he is the official messenger from Massasoit.

Massasoit's visit coincided with the harvest feast the English were already preparing. Edward Winslow, Resolved's stepfather, wrote about the visit in a letter he sent back to friends in England. That is how we know the two groups shared meals and games.

THANKSGIVING TRADITIONS AMONG THE WAMPANOAG PEOPLE

Wampanoag people give thanks every day. There is not one special day set aside especially for thanksgiving. They give thanks for everything—from the soil that grows crops to the moon in the sky. They believe that giving thanks is a special attitude and way of receiving the gifts of the Creator. Thanksgiving prayers look forward to the future; they uplift the heart and the mind, and they give solace to the grieving. Thanksgiving celebrations are held to honor ancestors, to celebrate a good crop, to signal the birth of a child, and to give thanks to the Creator, Kietan. There were "official" thanksgiving ceremonies for strawberries, green corn, and the harvest, which have been part of the Wampanoag tradition since the Creation. Feasting, games, singing, and dancing are part of these celebrations.

THANKSGIVING TRADITIONS AMONG THE ENGLISH COLONISTS

Many of the English colonists were determined to practice their religion the way they believed God commanded them to. That is primarily why they left England. They did not celebrate any religious holidays—not even Christmas or Easter. They celebrated only three kinds of holidays: the Sabbath, days of fasting, and days of thanksgiving. But these fasting and thanksgiving days were not regular. The leaders of the community declared the days when there were events or circumstances to celebrate or special favors to ask their god. Often, a day of thanksgiving followed one or more days of fasting. Days of thanksgiving were days of prayer, not days of feasting. According to the records of Plymouth Colony, the first fasting day was declared in 1623, two years after the harvest celebration we show in this book. It was followed by a day of thanksgiving because a drought was over and two ships carrying more colonists had arrived safely.

The English did, however, have a tradition of harvest celebrations. In the autumn, when the crops had been stored for the winter, there was often a big harvest meal on farms and in villages in England. The meal the settlers were preparing when Massasoit and his men arrived was such a harvest feast.

THE HISTORY OF THANKSGIVING AS A HOLIDAY

During the seventeenth century, individual colonies declared days of thanksgiving. By the eighteenth century, these days combined religious ideas with family gatherings and eating.

When the United States was a young country, the president would occasionally declare a national day of thanksgiving. One took place in 1789 when the Continental Congress was meeting. Another was held in 1812 to celebrate the end of a cholera epidemic.

Then, in 1841, New England historian Alexander Young published *Chronicles of the Pilgrim Fathers*. This book included a letter by Edward Winslow that mentioned the harvest feast of 1621. In a footnote, Dr. Young identified the event described by Winslow as the "first thanksgiving." That footnote caught the imagination of many people.

Earlier, Sarah Josepha Hale (the writer and editor who published "Mary Had a Little Lamb") began a campaign to have Thanksgiving declared a national holiday. Although Hale did not connect Thanksgiving with 1621 Plymouth, the long-ago harvest feast became associated with the modern holiday. She, among others, contributed to a myth that has continued through today.

On August 6, 1863, President Abraham Lincoln declared a thanksgiving day to celebrate the victories at Gettysburg and Vicksburg. That November, he called for another day of thanksgiving. That November thanksgiving day became the official holiday we celebrate today.

DINING

In 1621, the English harvest celebration lasted nearly a week. Massasoit and his 90 men were entertained for three days. There was not one feast, but many meals happening throughout the village. For some of these meals, the English ate with other English and the Wampanoag ate in their own encampment. At other times, natives were entertained by the English.

The English customarily ate three meals a day, the midday dinner being the most substantial. Ordinarily, the English ate indoors, sitting at a table, although children sometimes stood at a table. Celebratory feasts might take place indoors or outside; sometimes diners moved casually to and from the table, participating in other entertainments such as singing or sport. Some celebrations lasted into the next day.

Both the English and the Wampanoag maintained customs of honoring visiting dignitaries. In the photograph on pages 22–23, you will see actors playing the roles of the leaders of both communities. At the head of the table is William Brewster, who was the leader of the English congregation. On the left side of the table, starting at the top, is Captain Miles Standish (with his head bowed), who was the colony's military leader, and Resolved's stepfather, Edward Winslow, who spoke some Wampanoag. At the right side of the table, starting at the top, is Resolved's mother, Susannah Winslow (standing). Behind her (also standing) is George Soule, who was Edward Winslow's servant. Seated at the top is Squanto, who was the only surviving Patuxet Indian. He spoke English because he had been kidnapped and brought to Spain, then England. When, after seven years, he returned to his homeland, his people had all died in the plague of 1616–1618. Next is William Bradford, who was the governor; Sachem Massasoit; and Quadequina, Massasoit's brother. Standing behind Massasoit is Hobbamock, who was a *pniese*, or warrior counselor, and the interpreter who lived near the English settlement.

THE FOOD AT THE 1621 HARVEST CELEBRATION

According to the only written account, lots of wildfowl and venison were eaten in the course of the celebration. There is no record of what else was served, and food historians must surmise which other foods rounded out the tables. Native corn was a staple throughout the year for both the Wampanoag and the English. At harvest time, cod, eel, and shellfish were available, as were vegetables like cabbage, onions, and squash. Pies and sweets—if there were any— were likely served only to the very important diners. Dishes like cranberry sauce and mashed potatoes were not even invented yet.

A RECIPE: A POTTAGE OF NATIVE CORN WITH SPRING HERBS, ALSO CALLED SAMP

Here is a recipe for corn pudding that you can make. It was a very common food for the Wampanoag. They called it *nausamp*. The English adapted the word and called it "samp." *Nausamp* was made savory with broth or sweet with fruit. Native corn was a new food to the English, but they came to rely on it as a staple in their diet because it grew so successfully. English versions of this recipe often called for imported products like butter and sugar. This version uses common English garden herbs.

Hominy grits (*coarse grits are most authentic, but creamy grits will do*)
$1/2$ cup finely chopped parsley
$1/2$ cup finely chopped scallions

To cook the hominy, follow the directions on the package, but only add salt—no butter, cheese, or oil. When the grits are cooked, stir in the chopped parsley and scallions. (If the samp is too thick, you can add some boiling water.)

CLOTHING

The reenactment of the 1621 harvest feast was a massive undertaking. Hundreds of people were involved and worked for years getting ready for the three-day event that took place on October 7, 8, and 9, 2000. The clothing worn by the native people was made especially for this event by six native artisans. It took six months to make the headpieces composed of many kinds of feathers, and the deerskin leggings, fur mantles made of beaver, fox, skunk, and raccoon, woven sashes, and moccasins. The clothing was hand painted, sometimes using toothpicks. Stone, bone, wampum (quahaug, or clam, shells), and copper beads were used to make jewelry. Bows and war clubs were carved by hand. Porcupine quill embroidery decorated many pouches.

Plimoth Plantation's Wardrobe Department makes the clothing for the approximately 70 actors portraying the English colonists. Great attention is paid to every detail to make the reproduction clothing as much like the original seventeenth-century garments as possible. Machine sewing (a modern technique) is used to save time, but only in places where it won't show when the garment is finished. Seventeenth-century hand sewing techniques are used in every visible place, such as buttonholes, pleats, hems, and decorative trims. Almost all the fabric used is machine woven and chemically dyed (modern methods). However, each piece of cloth is carefully selected to represent the styles and colors available in the seventeenth century, when all cloth was handwoven and colored with natural dyes obtained from plant, animal, and mineral sources. The actors wear shoes that have been made by hand, using traditional seventeenth-century methods.

THE ACTORS

Graham Lebica played Resolved White. His mother works at Plimoth Plantation. He was seven years old when the photographs were taken and lives in Massachusetts. Graham likes archery, fishing, riding his scooter, reading, cooking, and writing stories. He would like to be an archaeologist when he gets older. The real Resolved White traveled to North America on the *Mayflower* with his mother and father. His brother, Peregrine White, was the first English child born in the colony. There is a picture of an interpreter playing Peregrine on the back cover. Resolved's father died and his mother married Edward Winslow.

Matthew Boardly played Dancing Moccasins. He is a Mashpee Wampanoag from Cape Cod, Massachusetts. Dancing Moccasins is a translation of Matt's Wampanoag name. Matt is very involved with the Wampanoag community. He is a traditional dancer at the annual Mashpee powwow held every July. He is a member of the Red Hawk singers, a youth group that performs at many powwows. Matt also makes many kinds of traditional crafts.

ABOUT THE WAMPANOAG INDIAN PROGRAM AT PLIMOTH PLANTATION

The Wampanoag Indian Program at Plimoth Plantation has an outdoor living history exhibit called Hobbamock's Homesite. It represents the seventeenth-century home of the native guide and interpreter who lived close to New Plymouth. The staff recreates seventeenth-century Wampanoag life by planting and tending corn, weaving mats and baskets, constructing *wetus* (houses), and preparing food. They do not role play, as most are from the Wampanoag Nation. People from other tribes also participate. The staff offers visitors the opportunity to hear history from a native perspective.

ABOUT PLIMOTH PLANTATION

Plimoth Plantation is the outdoor living history museum of seventeenth-century Plymouth, Massachusetts. The museum portrays life as it was led by the English colonists who came to North America in 1620, and by the Wampanoag, into whose territory the English settled. Visitors can explore Hobbamock's Homesite, the 1627 Pilgrim Village, *Mayflower II,* and the Crafts Center. At the 1627 Pilgrim Village, the modern visitor may talk with the interpreters as they go about their daily chores. Each interpreter has taken the role of a real-life Plymouth Colony resident.

For more information about the Wampanoag people and the English colonists, you can visit the Plimoth Plantation website at www.plimoth.org. Plimoth Plantation is open seven days a week from April through November. For more information call 508–746–1622.

For Further Reading about
Native Thanksgiving Traditions

This Circle of Thanks: Native American Poems and Songs of Thanksgiving by Joseph Bruchac, illustrated by Murv Jacob (Bridgewater Books, 1996).

Giving Thanks: A Native American Good Morning Message by Chief Jake Swamp, illustrated by Erwin Printup, Jr. (Lee & Low, 1995).

The Wampanoag and the First Thanksgiving (Everyday Learning Corp., 1997).

❧ GLOSSARY ❧

Broadly – By a great distance 9

Deer yard – A place where deer rest or eat. The underbrush is trampled down so it looks like a yard. 10

Draw – To take water out of a spring or well 14

Fetch – To get 16, 35

Fire pits – Cleared space to safely build a fire 24

Firs – Evergreen trees 24

Fitted up – Prepared 7

Fowling – Hunting wild birds 7

Hides – Skins of animals to be used for clothing and blankets 8

Homesite – Location of a person's home 6, 8, 10

Kietan – Wampanoag name for the Creator 6, 34

Kindling – Small twigs or sticks used to start a fire . .16

Musket – A large muzzle-loading gun 8

Musketeers – Soldiers armed with muskets 19

Pin game – A game with the object of swinging a hollow object and catching it with a spike 27

Pitching the bar – A game where one throws a big log as far as one can 29

Pluck – To pull the feathers off 12, 33

Pokanoket – One of more than 60 Wampanoag villages, located in what is now called Bristol, Rhode Island .13

Pompion – Squash or pumpkin 30

Rafters – Wooden beams that support a roof 7

Sachem – Chief or leader 11, 18

Samp – Porridge made from corn 30, 33

Stool ball – A game in which a ball is smacked with the arm and aimed at a stool. (It is like cricket without a bat.) 7

Storage pits – Mat-lined holes dug into the ground to hold dried food, such as corn and beans 6

Sup – To eat supper 30

Survey – To watch closely 9

Tongue – Language 9

Trace – Several ears of corn or bunches of onions braided together by the husks 7

Venison – The meat of deer 30, 31

Wunniook – Wampanoag word for "be well" 34